Fashion Design Secrets

By K. C. Kelley

The
Child's
World®
www.childsworld.com

Published in the United States of America by The Child's World®
1980 Lookout Drive • Mankato, MN 56003-1705
800-599-READ • www.childsworld.com

Thanks to Starshine Roshell for her fashion expertise.

ACKNOWLEDGMENTS

The Child's World® : Mary Berendes, Publishing Director

Produced by Shoreline Publishing Group LLC
President / Editorial Director: James Buckley, Jr.
Designer: Tom Carling, carlingdesign.com
Cover Art: Slimfilms
Copy Editor: Jim Gigliotti

Photo Credits:
Cover: Photos.com (main); iStock (insets)
Interior: AP/Wide World: 6, 24; Corbis: 18; Dreamstime.com
(photographers listed): João Continho 14, LuckyJ 16, Nicu Mircea
20, Kateryna Potrokhova 25, Daniel Sroga 7; The Metropolitan
Museum of Art, gift of Orme Wilson and R. Thornton Wilson,
in memory of their mother, Mrs. Caroline Schermerhorn Astor
Wilson, 1949 (49.3.25a, b and 49.3.28a, b), image © The Metropolitan
Museum of Art: 5; iStock: 8, 11, 19, 22, 26, 27; Photos.com: 9, 10, 15,
17, 21, 28; Shoreline Publishing Group 13.

LIBRARY OF CONGRESS CATALOG-IN-PUBLICATION DATA

Kelley, K. C.
   Fashion design secrets / by K.C. Kelley.
       p. cm. — (Reading rocks!)
   Includes bibliographical references and index.
   ISBN 978-1-60253-096-6 (library bound : alk. paper)
   1. Fashion design—Vocational guidance—Juvenile literature 2.
Fashion designers—Juvenile literature. I. Title. II. Series.

   TT507.R675 2008
   746.9'2—dc22

                                              2008004388

CONTENTS

STARTING OUT IN Fashion

Take a moment to look around you. Everyone is wearing clothes, right? All those shirts, pants, dresses, skirts, sweatshirts, and even caps were **designed** by someone. Whether clothes are plain or fancy, for wearing everyday or for a special event, they're all part of fashion.

The business of fashion design started around 1858. That's when an Englishman named Charles Worth started a shop in Paris. He made clothes for the rich and famous. People visiting the store saw models wearing Worth's designs. If they liked the clothes, customers could then order copies made to fit themselves. Soon, other designers and shops followed Worth's way of making and selling clothes. By the early 1900s, Paris was the home of *haute couture* (OHT kuh-TYOOR), or "high fashion."

In his Paris store, Charles Worth created many beautiful gowns like these.

Celebrities like Jennifer Lopez and Marc Anthony often show off the finest in high fashion.

Fashion companies today make millions of dollars designing and making clothes. People working at these companies work with colors, shapes, and styles. They choose from different fabrics and materials to make new clothing ideas. The creative people who come up with the ideas for new clothes are called fashion designers. They create the styles that people will wear. Designers also choose what fabrics are used and what colors will be popular.

There are three main areas of fashion design. Fashion designers usually **specialize** in one type of clothing. *High fashion* includes very expensive, one-of-a-kind outfits. These are sometimes made for just one person to wear—only once! Some high-fashion clothes are made just for movie or music stars.

Ready-to-wear clothes are less expensive than high-fashion ones. These styles are made for more people to buy. But these clothes are still made with very nice fabrics that are often too expensive for many people to buy.

Mass-market clothes are made in very large numbers and cost much less. Most of the clothes that everyday people wear are mass-market.

Ready-to-wear clothes are often worn by women who want to be stylish and comfortable.

A fashion designer's first tools are a pencil and a pad. The sketches designers create with these tools will become new designs.

With all the types of clothing in the world, fashion companies must be organized. Most companies focus on just one type of clothing. Larger companies, however, might make clothes for lots of different people. These companies hire designers who can create many different styles.

Fashion designers work with other people in a company to determine the types of clothes people are likely to buy in the coming year.

They must work many months ahead of when the clothes will actually be sold. That's because designing and making clothes takes a long time. For instance, a designer might work all winter on clothes that won't be sold until summertime!

Types of Clothing

Most designers and companies work in one main area of fashion. These are the most popular areas of the fashion world:

- Women's wear
- Teens
- Sportswear
- Underwear
- Bridal wear
- Menswear
- Children's
- Outerwear
- Evening wear*
- Accessories**

* Fancy clothes such as tuxedos or ball gowns.
** Extra items to wear or use, such as purses, hats, scarves, or bags.

Most fashion designers learn how to do their jobs at fashion schools. They study art, design, fabrics, sewing, and other areas. A fashion designer must have a great sense of style and understand how color and **line** work on a person's body. They have to be very good at drawing, too.

At school, young designers draw ideas for new styles. They might

Sew What?

Even the most famous fashion designers began their careers sewing. If you want to create clothing, you should know how to sew. Once you learn to use a sewing machine, you can make almost anything— from a pillowcase to a formal gown!

change a drawing many times before they're happy with it. When ready, a designer will actually cut fabrics and sew together the pieces for their new design. At the end of their schooling, designers have a **portfolio** of their work. This shows companies the kinds of clothes the designer is good at creating.

Most designers start out as assistants. They might work for a large company or for a small **studio**.

Student designers cut fabrics for their ideas after carefully measuring each piece.

HERE COMES THE Fashion!

How do fashion designers create their masterpieces? It takes a lot of imagination, planning, skill, and hard work. First, designers watch the world around them. They look at the colors, shapes, and fabrics that people are wearing—and then they try to guess what those same people will want to wear in the future. Designers look at fashion magazines to see which styles are popular. They visit stores to see other designers' ideas. And they always keep their eyes out for new kinds of fabrics.

Since fashion changes with every season, most companies put out new styles twice a year—in the spring and in the fall. But just when one season's **collection** has been designed, sewn, and shipped to stores, it's time to start designing the next season's clothes!

A designer's collection includes all the clothes that he or she has designed for that season.

Fashion magazines feature beautiful models wearing all the latest styles.

Fashion designers use pencils, pens, and colored markers to create sketches of new clothing.

Let's follow along as fashion designers turn their ideas into clothes for you to wear. First, designers sketch their ideas onto large paper pads. They try different shapes, lengths, and cuts. They might play around with colors or add details like buttons or flaps. This is the fun part for most designers—when their imaginations can run wild!

Designers must always keep their customers in mind. If a design is too silly or uncomfortable, people won't want to buy it. Designers work with lots of fabrics to decide which ones work best with their ideas. They **drape** the fabrics on **dummies**. This helps designers see how different fabrics lay on a person's body. Out of all this thinking, drawing, and draping comes ideas for some great new clothes.

Fashion dummies are made in the shape of people.

The muslin is loosely draped and stitched on the dummy to see how the new design fits.

The next step is to make a **sample** of the design. Some designers create samples themselves, but many work with **seamstresses**. First, fabric is cut to the right size and shape. Then the pieces are loosely sewn together. Sewing the sample loosely lets the designer make adjustments. This early-stage piece is sometimes called a **muslin** after the inexpensive fabric it's made with.

The designer will work with the muslin to make the piece look just right. She might make the dress longer or change the shape of the sleeve or neck. She might take it apart and put it back together many times before it's finally done.

Then it's time to use the real fabric to make a full sample. The designer also chooses buttons, ribbons, and other pieces of trim.

After choosing the fabric, the designer sews some pieces together to make a sample.

Designers measure and check each part to make sure everything fits together correctly.

Often a designer will put the handmade sample on a real-life model. Seeing how a person moves in the piece shows the designer a lot. Does the dress move well

There are hundreds of different fabrics—and colors—for designers to choose from!

around the model's legs? Can her arms move well in the sleeves? Is the neck too high or too low? From the original idea, many changes have been made.

Once the designer is happy with the sample, another worker makes a **pattern** out of paper. This is a bit like a jigsaw puzzle of all the parts. This pattern will be used to make sure that every copy of the piece of clothing is the same.

Some sewing stores sell patterns that you can use to make your own clothes.

Large factories like this one can create lots of copies of a piece of clothing in a short time.

The paper pattern is used to cut the fabric into the right shapes. Then the pieces are sewn together, either with large machines (for mass-market clothes) or by hand (for haute couture outfits). Large factories can turn out hundreds or thousands of pieces in just hours.

It has taken many hours of hard work, and lots of new ideas and changes, but the fashion designer has done it. She has taken her new idea from some pencil sketches and turned them into clothing for people to wear.

But the work of the fashion designer is far from over!

Ecofashion

Like many people, fashion designers today are concerned with the **environment**. Some designers are starting to use materials that are recycled or that don't harm the environment. Designer Lara Miller, for example, makes clothes from the scraps of old T-shirts. She also makes clothes from bamboo, a type of grass that grows quickly.

3

THE SHOW AND
the Store

All that hard work is just a part of the designer's job. She and other designers will make many new pieces for their fashion company. Together, these new clothes make up a "line."

How do designers choose which clothes to include in their company's lines? First, they talk to the owners of the stores in which the clothes will be sold. These people know their customers. They know the types of clothes that their customers will buy. Designers also try to follow **trends**, which are a little like fads. For example, perhaps bright colors are the trend for spring, while denim clothing is popular in the fall.

Most companies tell people about their new lines by holding fashion shows. These can be very **glamorous** events. The most important fashion shows are held in New York City, London, and Paris. Hundreds of people from the fashion world come together

Just Showing Off

Most fashion shows feature clothes that people might see in stores. But some shows feature clothes that are just wonderful creations designers want to show off. These pieces might be one-of-a-kind dresses or amazing outfits. There might be strange fabrics or wild shapes. These are not clothes that you'll see in stores, but when these artful pieces hit the runway, fashion fans take notice!

to watch models show off the new clothes. Dressed in all types of clothes, the models walk down a **runway**. Sometimes they pose or twirl. Fashion fans fill the seats along the sides of the runway. Bright lights and loud music make the shows fun and exciting.

Models walk down the runway, showing off a company's latest fashions.

People working in clothing stores make sure that the designers' work is ready for customers.

After being featured in fashion shows, clothes are often advertised in magazines. They soon arrive in stores, where customers try them on . . . and hopefully buy them! As pieces begin to sell, the designer is still working. She studies information from the stores to see which clothes are selling well. Sometimes a magazine or Web site will write a **review** of the new clothes. Do people like them? Do they dislike them? The designer wants to know! All this information will help her shape the next line of clothes.

Soon it's back to the drawing pad for the fashion designer. She and other people at her company must begin coming up with new designs for the season ahead.

After the clothes are in the stores, it's back to the drawing pad for designers!

The world of fashion is an exciting, creative, and busy place. If you love clothes and fashion, there are many ways in which you can join this world. Becoming a fashion designer is one way, of course. Practice your drawing skills by creating dresses, pants, shirts . . . or whatever.

Trying on clothes at a store is a fun way to discover fashion trends.

Ask your parents to help you get some fabrics, and start experimenting with different ideas. It would also be good to learn how to sew. Knowing how clothes are put together can give you new ideas for designs.

Reading about clothing and fashion can also be helpful. Your knowledge of fashion might help you sell clothes to stores. And as you get older, you might even work at a clothing store to learn more about what customers like to buy.

What's the best way to enter the world of fashion? Just open your closet and start having fun with your own clothes!

Create your own portfolio of fashion designs! Keep all of your best drawings in a notebook and show them to your friends.

GLOSSARY

collection a group of clothes put out by a fashion company

designed created new types of clothing ideas by sketching and sewing

drape laying cloth on a dummy or a person to see how a piece of clothing might look

dummies soft, headless statues used to model and fit clothing

environment the land, air, plants, and water all around us

glamorous very fancy

haute couture French words meaning "high fashion"

line how clothing fits on a person's body; also, a group of clothes put out by a fashion company

muslin an early version of a sample

pattern the paper outline used to show the shape or shapes that will make up a piece of clothing

portfolio a collection of drawings by a fashion designer

review an article that gives someone's opinion about an event or a line of clothing

runway the long walkway used in fashion shows

sample the first version of a piece, before it has been perfected and sold to customers

seamstresses people who sew

specialize to focus on just one type of thing (in this case, one type of clothing)

studio a small design company or a small group of designers

trends fads that show the kind of clothing most people are wearing

FIND OUT MORE

BOOKS

Different Like Coco
By Elizabeth Matthews, Candlewick, 2007
Read about Coco Chanel, one of the world's most famous
fashion designers.

Fashion Design: Draw It!
By Tiffany Peterson, Heinemann Library, 2008
This book helps you practice your design talents by creating a
different outfit for each decade of the 20th century.

I Want to Be a Fashion Designer
By Stephanie Maze, Harcourt Brace, 2000
Visit designers, see how different types of clothes are made,
and learn how a fashion show works.

WEB SITES

Visit our Web site for lots of links about fashion and fashion
design: www.childsworld.com/links

Note to Parents, Teachers, and Librarians: We routinely check our Web links to
make sure they're safe, active sites—so encourage your readers to check them out!

INDEX

K. C. Kelley has written many books for young readers on a wide variety of topics, from astronauts to baseball to robots. He doesn't wear fancy clothes when he writes, but his daughter Katie loves to try on all sorts of clothes.